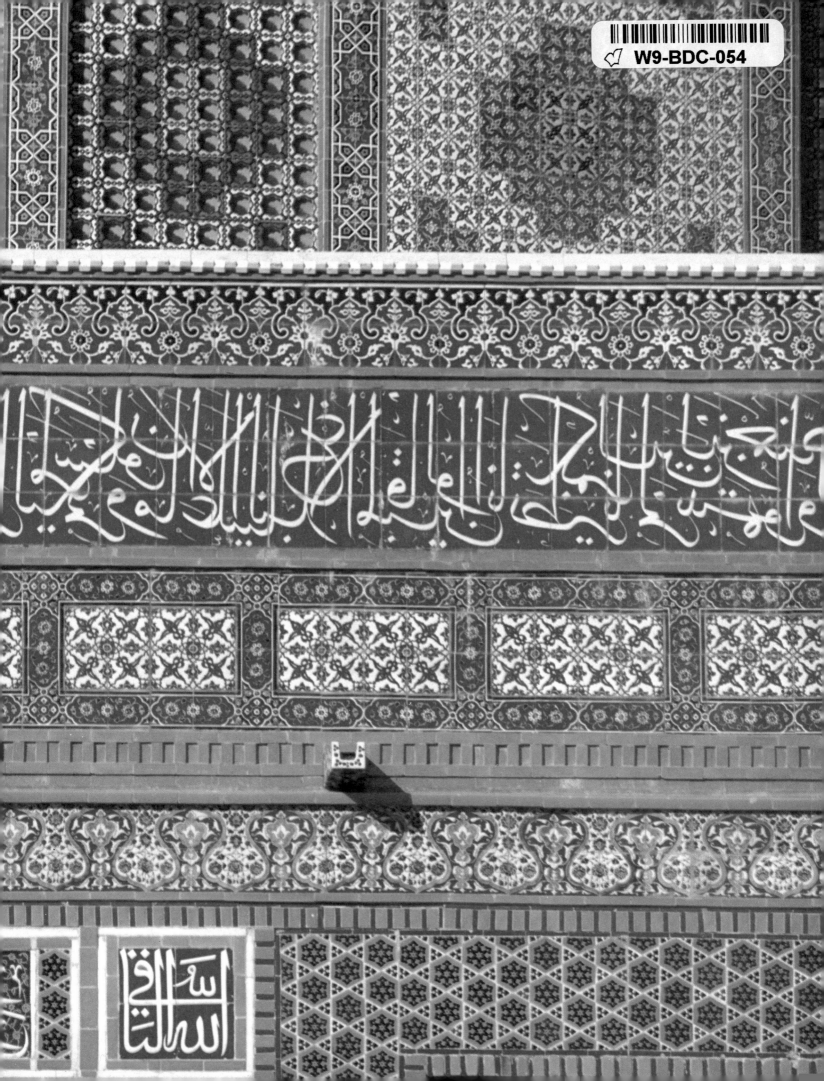

24 Iyar 5746

Presented to: Michael Mendelsohn

In Honor of His
Religious School Graduation

Oceanside Jewish Center

Chana Simches
Educational Director

This book was devised and produced by
Multimedia Publications (UK) Ltd

Editor: Marilyn Inglis
Production: Karen Bromley
Design: John Strange
Picture Research: Tessa Paul

First published in the United States of
America 1985 by Gallery Books, an imprint of
W. H. Smith Publishers Inc., 112 Madison
Avenue, New York, NY 10016

ISBN 0 8317 5017 0

Typeset by Flowery
Origination by York House Graphics Ltd
Printed in Italy by Sagdos

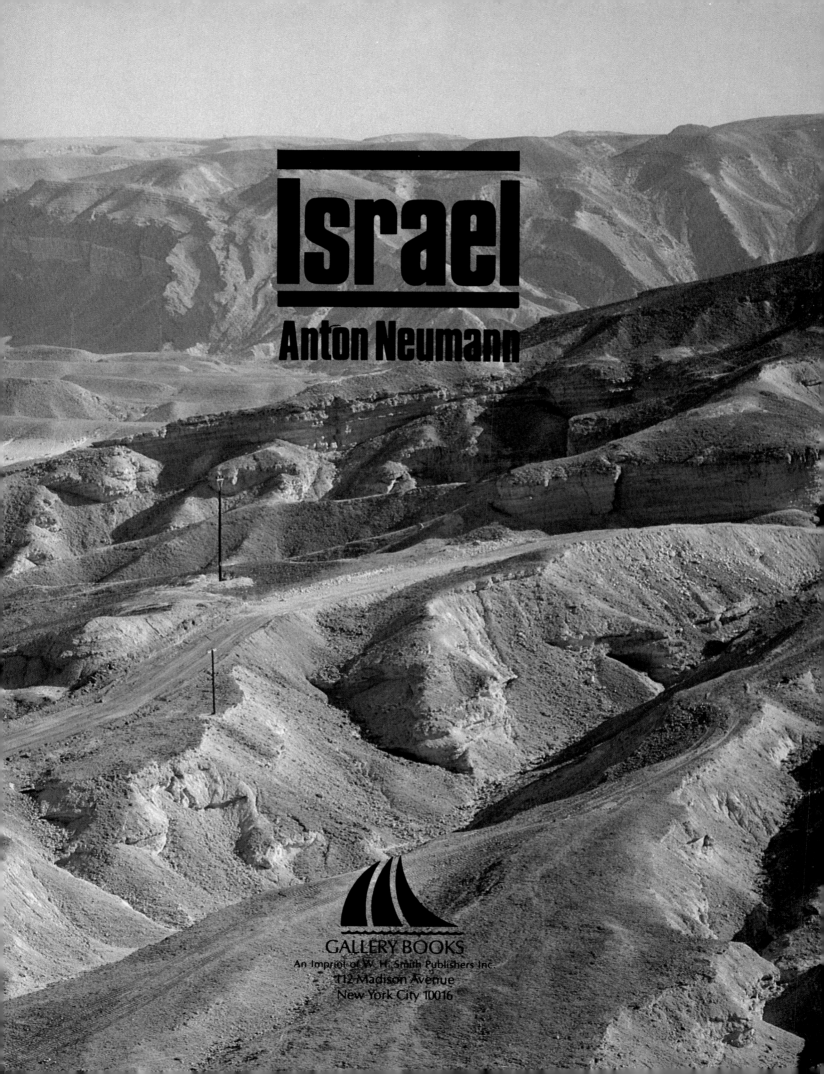

Israel

Anton Neumann

GALLERY BOOKS
An Imprint of W. H. Smith Publishers Inc.
112 Madison Avenue
New York City 10016

Endpapers Mosaic at the Dome of the Rock, Jerusalem.

Half title page An old Menorah.

Title page The Negev Desert.

Contents page Salt formations in the Dead Sea.

Credits page Candles are constantly lit at the graves of Israeli soldiers.

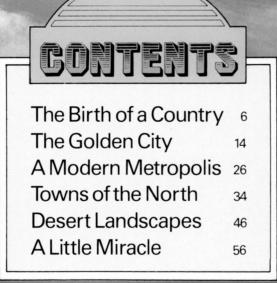

CONTENTS

CHAPTER 1

The Birth of a Country

Israel is a country where ancient and modern traditions rub shoulders casually in the street. It is a country whose history stretches into the dawn of modern civilization and yet, as a modern state, it has only recently left its adolescence behind. For the visitor to Israel, this strange combination provides exciting and unexpected experiences. One can walk out of a modern bank, equipped with all of today's electronic wizardry, into the hustle and bustle of an Arab "shouk" that has changed very little in the last hundred years. Around almost every street corner one finds signs of Israel's youth and vitality contrasting with its ancient and holy past.

The youth and vitality are not illusory. Israel is not only young in years but also in the age of her population; almost 40 per cent are under the age of 17. Youth, however, does not always breed politeness and the visitor will make a time-consuming mistake should he decide to stand in line at the bus stop or supermarket. The young Israeli has, for this very reason, been nicknamed a "sabra"; a native fruit which is prickly on the outside but with a sweet and soft center. The problem, of course, is how to get to that center! Once there however, the average Israeli is indeed both warm and friendly and one should not be surprised to find oneself invited back home to meet the family and partake of the evening meal.

Traveling within Israel is an exhilarating experience. In spite of the overcrowded coach stations, buses run on time and are very cheap. Coaches are nearly always full and literally buzz with excited conversation and the din of the radio. Israel also has a unique form of transport in the shape of the "sherut". These are shared taxis which charge a set price and travel on the main inter-city routes. Beware, however, the drivers are fast and are not for those with a weak heart.

Below left The headdress is part of the traditional Arab national costume and is still worn today by many Arabs. Although it is a decorative garment it also provides essential protection from the heat of the sun and from the ferocity of the desert wind.

Below right Prayer is an integral part of Muslim life. From the minarets of the numerous mosques in Israel the visitor will often hear the traditional chant calling Muslims to afternoon and evening payers.

Bottom Israel's a country with a diversity of styles of cuisine imported by her wide variety of immigrants. However, this Arab dish, although in a modern container, has probably been served in this land for centuries.

The visitor has not always been able to travel with the ease of the modern tourist. For centuries the "super-powers" of the region have fought over and around the country, and for most of her 5000 years of history she has been a vassal state. The state was first founded in approximately 1500 BC, when Jewish slaves under the leadership of Moses escaped from the Pharaohs. After 40 years of wandering in the wilderness they eventually entered Canaan, as the land was then known, and after many battles succeeded in establishing the first Jewish state.

In spite of all their traumas, the Israelites have many remarkable and significant achievements to their name. They built the temple, which by all accounts was a splendid architectural development. They had many brilliant victories over their enemies. King David was able to end the

Philistine threat, and under the peaceful rule of King Solomon, the Israelite Kingdom was able to prosper and become an important economic and trading country. Under the Maccabees, Hellenistic domination of the country was overthrown. Even against the armies of mighty Rome, the Jews were able to score some significant victories, and for three short years under the charismatic leadership of Bar Kochba, the Israelites were actually able to gain their independence from Roman rule.

Most importantly perhaps, the Israelites developed a unique moral and ethical code, large parts of which form the foundation of both Christianity and Islam. They also provided the world, and Western civilization in particular, with one of the most important of holy books, the Old Testament. The first five books of the Old Testament are known to Jews as the Torah.

In the period after the birth of Christ, the land of Israel gradually lost all semblance of its independence. It became a province, firstly of the Christian Byzantine empire, then of the Moslem empire, then of the Crusaders and the Mamelukes, and finally part of the Ottoman Turkish empire. Throughout the period Jews lived within the land, and in Safed, Tiberias, Hebron and Jerusalem there existed thriving, although impoverished, religious communities.

It was not until late in the nineteenth century that the roots of the present Republic of Israel were first laid. In Austria in 1894 a young Jewish journalist called Herzl was so enraged by the anti-semitism displayed in the notorious Dreyfus trial that he was moved to write a book proposing the establishment of an independent Jewish state as a solution to the horrors of European racism. His ideas fell on fertile ground and in 1897 the first Zionist Congress was held. In little more than 50 years Herzl's dreams blossomed into reality, and in 1948 the new state was born.

But the birth was not without its complications. Over the centuries many peoples had made Israel their home. They resented and felt threatened by the return of the Jewish people from their exile. The British, who in 1918 had replaced the Turkish administration, were committed to the establishment of a Jewish national home, but they were also keen to appease nascent Arab nationalism. In keeping with its turbulent past, the period of British rule was characterized by riots, strikes and massacres. Finally, with the end of World War II, the British wiped their hands of the matter, throwing the whole problem into the lap of the United Nations. In a nail-biting vote, the UN resolved to divide the disputed

Below Per head of population Israelis consume more chickens than any other nation in the world. It is not therefore surprising that chicken farming is big business. No doubt the proverbial medical qualities of the family 'chicken soup' are partly responsible for the chicken's success.

land into two small states; one Jewish and one Arab. The delighted Jewish community immediately accepted the plan, and in a moving ceremony created the first independent Jewish state since the time of the Romans.

Yet in many ways Israel's problems were only just starting. The infant state was attacked by all of its Arab neighbors, who did not accept the United Nations' decision. To the amazement of the onlooking world, Jews who had previously been known for their quiet and passive ways displayed all the military skills of their biblical ancestors, and miraculously the state survived the vicious onslaught. Since then, Israel has fought five wars, although there has been an extremely high cost to pay both in money and in blood.

With the exception of Egypt, with whom an historic peace has been made, Israel remains surrounded by hostile states. For such a small state this constant threat to her security has necessitated the establishment of a formidable army through which most of Israel's citizens have passed at one stage in their lives.

Yet within Israel's borders, Arabs, Jews and Christians live in relative harmony, all enjoying religious and democratic freedoms. In Jerusalem for instance, all three religions live peacefully side by side. In the space of an hour the visitor can see priests carrying a wooden cross down the Via de la Rosa, Jews celebrating a boy's Barmitzvah in front of the Wailing Wall, and Moslems congregating for afternoon prayers at the Dome of the Rock. In Bethlehem much preparation goes into the elaborate Christmas preparations. But it is a Jewish official who is responsible for its organization and the delicate negotiations between the Roman Catholics, The Eastern Orthodox and the Armenian Christians, all of whom celebrate Christmas on different days. It is this tolerance of other religions and beliefs that helps to make Israel the exciting multi-cultural society known and loved by pilgrims and tourists alike.

To Israelis the existence of their small but strong army is a sad fact of life. Few families have been spared the tragedy of losing one of their loved ones, and each and every family is acutely aware of the constant

security threat posed to the country by her hostile neighbors. Israel has fought five bloody wars, and in order to insure her survival has had to develop a powerful and sophisticated armed force. The armed forces are based on a small standing army which in times of trouble is expanded by the calling up of reservists. At the age of 18 young Israeli men and women have to sacrifice three years of their youth to the army, and even after having returned to civilian life they are required to give the army at least one month's service – a service known as "milluim" – each year.

In spite of its strength and military success, the Israeli army is quite different from those of other western states. There is a degree of casualness to it that will surprise the visitor accustomed to the spick and span usually associated with military life. Soldiers are frequently seen hitching lifts from passing cars, their boots covered in desert sand and their green khaki uniforms soiled by a hard day's work. The Israeli army is also unique in that it relies heavily on the contribution of women. In the 1948 War of Independence, women fought side

by side with the men. The modern Israeli army does not require women to become front line troops, although they receive much of the necessary training. Instead they provide many of the supporting services, which although not as glamorous are certainly just as essential to Israel's survival.

The armed forces also serve a useful function. They provide the "melting pot" from which the Israeli nation has been formed. In 1948 when Israel became an independent state, she opened her doors to those Jews still living in the "diaspora". Jews whose families had been destroyed in the war and who had become homeless refugees flooded into the country together with entire Jewish communities who had for centuries lived as second class citizens in Arab countries. Although Jews, these new immigrants came from very different backgrounds and cultures. The Jews from Yemen for instance, had lived for many years isolated from the western world and world Jewry. When Israeli planes landed to return them to their homeland, they thought they were the giant eagles referred

Facing page above A religious Jew contemplates the new day as he prepares himself for morning prayers. It is necessary for at least ten men to be present before the service can begin, but this is rarely a problem in Israel.

Facing page below Mea-Shearim in Jerusalem is the home of one of the most religious Jewish sects in Israel and the graffiti on the wall was written by them. They believe that the state of Israel should come into existence only when the Messiah returns. In spite of their radical views they remain an accepted and integral part of the Jewish state.

Above Israel remembers her dead. This memorial is dedicated to the memory of the six million Jews who were murdered during the Second World War. Yad Vashem in Jerusalem is the most significant memorial to the holocaust dead. It is also a research center and contains many important documents and books relating to Nazi Germany.

Left Adding yet another facet to the variety of Israel's Jewish community, the Falasha Jews arrived from Ethiopia in 1985.

11

to in the Bible and indeed there are stories of small camp fires being lit inside the planes by the Yemenites in order to cook their food. These sharp and contrasting backgrounds continue to cause many problems within Israel. By throwing these different cultures together in a common cause the army has been a unifying force and has greatly assisted in lessening the many social and economic problems which have resulted from Israel's multi-cultural society.

While the differing cultures and backgrounds of Israel's inhabitants may create some problems, they also provide the visitor with a wide range of cultural entertainment. One can sit in Tel Aviv's modern concert hall listening to Mozart being performed by one of the world's best orchestras; or watch a modern dance which incorporates ancient Yemenite choreography; or if one is of more boisterous spirit then join a folk dancing group for a lively and exhausting evening. Israeli food is also affected by the cultural mix of the country's inhabitants. It's possible to sit down to a traditional Hungarian meal with its hearty "goulash" and thick beefy soups; or to taste the more spicy and exotic food of the Moroccan and Arab Jews; or sample the well-known delights of Chinese cuisine which may even be kosher! Many restaurants serve only kosher food, prepared under strict religious supervision. Milk and meat cannot be served together and the visitor may often find that the ancient religious laws assist modern dietary convention in preventing him from feasting on a rich creamy dessert!

For the serious drinker Israel is a disappointment. Jews are not heavy drinkers and Islam actually forbids the consumption of alcohol. But there are a few bars in Tel Aviv and Jerusalem where the really desperate can quench their thirst. For the coffee drinker however, Israel offers a wide range of different coffees from the almost undrinkable "botz" to the more sophisticated "cappuccino". There are numerous cafés and the visitor will quickly find that at the end of a hard day's touring one of the most pleasant ways in which to relax is to slump down over a good strong coffee and watch those who still have energy rush past as they go about their frenetic business.

Right Off to work in style! Israel is still a very young and relatively poor country. Hard work is something that all her citizens are well accustomed to. It is not unusual to meet people who have a full time day job which they somehow manage to combine with an arduous evening job. In spite of it all, Israelis seem to remain fresh and vital.

Far left In the harsh climate of the Middle East every flower is a minor miracle. Nevertheless with a combination of encouragement, hard work and loving care, Israelis manage to beautify their gardens and public parks with a colorful range of plants.

Left Fashion is a successful and important sector of the Israeli economy. In 1982 it earned more than $100 million in export orders. Not surprisingly in such a hot climate Israel leads the world in beach-wear design.

Below Small street shops are a common feature on Israeli street corners.

Overleaf An aerial view of the Temple Mount in Jerusalem. To the right is the octagonal Dome of the Rock. At the top center is the Wailing Wall and to the left the Al Aqsa Mosque. The history of the Temple Mount is deeply woven into both Judaism and Islam. It is believed to be the site where God tested Abraham by ordering him to kill his son Isaac. It is also the site where Mohammed is supposed to have ascended to heaven.

14

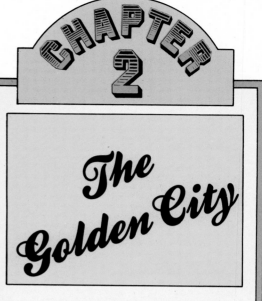

CHAPTER 2

The Golden City

Jerusalem contains many of the magical qualities that make Israel such an enchanting country for the visitor. It sits perched high on the Judaean hills; a spiritual oasis in the surrounding desert landscape. It has a most equable climate, and enjoys a dry heat, even on the hottest day, with cool and pleasant nights.

In spite of the turmoil of its past, in which the city has more than once been completely destroyed, Jerusalem survives today as the cultural and political center of Israel, and to many peoples as the spiritual center of the world. This centrality is reflected in the every day life of Jerusalemites, or Yerushalmis, as they're colloquially known. In the street one can hear myriad languages spoken, and see a vast array of different cultures, religions and sects going about their daily business.

It is the old city that lies at the heart of Jerusalem. The impressive walls that surround the city were built by the Turks in 1537, but the city's history goes back much further than this. It was mentioned by the Egyptians in the nineteenth century BC and Abraham's association with the city has been traced back to the eighteenth century BC. Nevertheless the city only became part of the Israelite kingdom in the tenth century BC when it was assaulted and conquered by King David.

Jerusalemites are proud of their city and are not reticent in praising its many qualities. The visitor will find himself besieged by an army of would-be guides touting for business. Jerusalem's charm however, is that it lends itself to the explorer who is willing to lose himself down quiet alleys which often feel as though they belong to the previous century. No matter how lost though, no visitor can miss the Dome of the Rock, or Golden Mosque, which dominates the city. Architecturally it is the most impressive sight in Jerusalem

Above According to legend the original cupola of the Golden Mosque was covered with more than 10 000 sheets of pure gold. The building collapsed in AD 1016 and the present roof, completed in 1963, is made of gilded aluminum sheets.

and is substantially the same building as that built in AD 691. Legend has it that Mohammed left earth for heaven from precisely this spot, and visitors can see an imprint in the rock that is believed to be the footprint of Mohammed himself.

The site on which the Golden Mosque is built is also holy to the Jewish religion. It was on this site that Solomon's temple was built, and although it was destroyed by the Babylonians there are remains of the second re-built temple. The best-known site is the Wailing Wall. Its stones are believed to weep for the persecuted and exiled Children of Israel. Prior to 1967, the wall lay within Jordanian territory, and it was not until after the Six Day War and the re-unification of Jerusalem that Jews were again able to pray at their most holy site.

Today Jews congregate in the large forecourt in front of the wall, and if one is interested in philosophical debate just linger a little while and you're bound to be approached by a religious Jew, prepared to argue well into the night in an attempt to save your soul!

Christianity is of course well represented in this holy city. When the Roman empire began to convert to Christianity in the fourth century AD, its first Christian Queen, Queen Helena, visited Jerusalem and marked out the route followed by Jesus as he walked to his crucifixion. At the main points along the route, and indeed elsewhere in the city, churches were built: the most important is the Church of the Holy Sepulcher. This marks the last 5 of the 14 Stations of the Cross. The Holy Sepulcher

contains within it numerous chapels, each run by a separate Christian denomination. These "rights" holders, as they are known, have difficulty in agreeing with each other, so much so that under the Turkish administration Moslems were accepted as mediators and it was they who kept the keys to the Church. Under the British things were not much better, and as a result of the bickering, repairs to the church after the damage caused in the 1927 earthquake have only very recently been completed.

The old city is very much more than a collection of religious and historical sites. It is a city alive with people working, playing and enjoying themselves. In the bazaars that criss-cross the city visitors can purchase an unusually broad selection of goods. Under the city's oriental vaulted markets the

choice ranges from everyday groceries to ebony, beautifully inlaid with mother-of-pearl, handwoven rugs and embroidered dresses. It is in the bazaars that one senses the excitement and vitality of the city as shopkeepers, priests, rabbis and tourists are jostled down its narrow paths.

Jerusalem does not end when one finally emerges from within the walls of the old city. The new city has a charm of its own with the buildings clad in attractive pink Jerusalem stone. The town center has a good selection of shops and restaurants. As one would expect from a cosmopolitan city such as Jerusalem, one can indulge in a wide range of gastronomic delights.

An old Jewish tale says that if two Jews are together in a room there will be at least three points of view. In Jerusalem, the

Above left The entrance to the Golden Mosque.

Above right The interior of the mosque is beautifully although simply decorated. The center is dominated by the rock which is supposed to be the summit of Mount Moriah and the site of the altars of the first and second Temples.

political center of the country, this is particularly true. Israel's parliament, the Knesset, seems to be in constant debate. Elected by a system of proportional representation, Israeli governments are dependent on a coalition of smaller parties in order to stay in power. Surprisingly though, this has always provided stable government, although the most recent elections have created problems that will test to the utmost the political ingenuity of Israel's leadership.

The Knesset building is itself an architecturally striking sight. Built in 1966, it is a long, low structure of pink Jerusalem stone. Within its large reception hall hang three magnificent Chagall tapestries. Close to the Knesset lies the Israel Museum, the striking Shrine of the Book and the Givat

Ram campus of the Hebrew University. All three are open to the visitor, but it is perhaps the Shrine of the Book, with its priceless biblical scrolls, that attracts the most attention. The Givat Ram campus is only part of the Hebrew University. While the city remained divided the Mount Scopus campus was unusable and so the Givat Ram site was developed as an alternative. Now that Jerusalem is once again a unified city, the Mount Scopus campus is again in use and is well worth a visit.

Leaving Jerusalem is a painful experience both for the visitor and the Jerusalemite himself. One can easily understand the emotions of the Israelites, who having been carried into exile by the Babylonians in 587 BC, cried out:

If I forget thee, O Jerusalem, let my right hand forget her cunning. If I do not remember thee, let my tongue cleave to the roof of my mouth. (Psalms 137)

In contrast however, the modern visitor should have no difficulty in returning whenever he so desires.

Close to Jerusalem lies Bethlehem. Its history is closely connected with the nearby metropolis. Today it is a smallish town largely inhabited by Christian Arabs who work as skilled artisans and craftsmen. The township is the biblical site of the burial of Jacob's young wife Rachel, and there are also many other biblical connections. It is however to Christianity that Bethlehem is of most importance. It was here that Jesus was born and visited by the three wise

Left A view of the interior of the Church of the Holy Sepulcher. Although seriously damaged by fire in 1808 and by an earthquake in 1927 the present-day church is identical to the Crusader building completed in 1149. In the center of the church lies the tomb that is believed to be the chamber in which Christ was entombed.

Below Part of the Easter procession. Armenian priests follow in the footsteps of Jesus, as they walk along the Via Dolorosa. On Fridays the visitor can still see Franciscan monks retracing Christ's footsteps while carrying a wooden cross similar in size and weight to the original.

men. The site of his birth is now marked by a church, the Basilica of the Nativity which was built in 614 AD and has been altered very little since.

In the fields that surround Bethlehem, shepherds still pasture their flocks, and if it weren't for the occasional passing car it would be possible to imagine oneself back in the holy land of biblical times.

Right A view of the Russian Orthodox Church of Mary Magdalene. Built in 1880 and given to White Russian nuns in 1907, the church marks the site at which the head of John the Baptist is said to have been found.

Below The Wailing Wall is the holiest of Jewish sites. It symbolizes both the continuity of Jewish existence in Jerusalem and the destruction of the Temple itself. It is a custom for Jewish visitors to write their requests on paper which are then inserted into the cracks of the wall.

Above right Since the re-unification of Jerusalem in 1967 the houses which were built right up to the wall have been cleared, and the forecourt created is now used for religious celebrations. The most common of these is of course the Barmitzvah, at which the boy is welcomed into adulthood by reading from the Torah.

Below right Religious Jews congregate at the wall and there is in fact a synagogue hidden at its side. One can frequently observe Jews deep in prayer and oblivious to the outside world. Ironically perhaps, they are not allowed to enter the temple complex itself since the exact site of the ark, which is considered holy ground, remains unknown.

Right Resembling a tree stump, the Kennedy Memorial symbolizes a life cut off in its prime. An eternal flame within commemorates the former US president and his brother, Robert Kennedy. The memorial was erected with the contributions of American citizens.

Below The wrought iron entrance of the Knesset is the work of the Israeli sculptor, Polombo. Opposite the entrance stands a giant bronze menorah. Executed by the sculptor Benno Elkan, it was a gift from the British government. The scenes engraved on it depict events from Jewish history.

Left Visible on the horizon are the modern buildings of the Hebrew University. The university provides a high standard of academic learning and is open to men and women of all races and nationalities. It has two campuses, one in Givat Ram (near the Knesset), the other high up on Mount Scopus.

Below A book market in Jerusalem. Israelis are avid readers and publishers have little problem in selling their books. Indeed, Israel has one of the highest rates of book production, per head of population, in the world.

Right Part of the relief engraved on the outside of the "Grotto of the Milk" in Bethlehem. Tradition holds that while Mary was suckling the infant Jesus a few drops of her milk fell at this spot and turned the rock into soft white stone.

Below left Although Israel is a modern country, old traditions survive. Here a water-carrier passes through the markets in the old City of Jerusalem. Less than a hundred years ago this would have been an everyday sight throughout the country.

Below right The Arab "shouk" in the Old City of Jerusalem retains all the characteristics of ages gone by. The visitor can enjoy the noise and bustle of the shouk's narrow alleyways while still discovering interesting and attractive bargains.

Facing page Bethlehem has an old world charm of its own. In Hebrew, the word Bethlehem translates into "House of Bread" and in Arabic into "House of Meat". These names are supposed to refer to the fertility of the surrounding region which is still clearly visible today.

CHAPTER 3

A Modern Metropolis

Tel Aviv is in very many ways a complete contrast to Jerusalem. It's a modern commercial city lying on the flat and fertile coastal plain and has a population today in excess of 400 000, making it the largest city in Israel. Jaffa, which merges into Tel Aviv, has an ancient history, but Tel Aviv was only founded in 1909. Its name translates into English as "Hill of Spring", and was intended by its founders to symbolize the "Old New Land" of Herzl's dreams. During World War I, the Turks expelled the Jewish settlers but with the disintegration of the Ottoman empire and the victory of the British, Jews were once again allowed to return to the land.

Tel Aviv is also the most fashionable of Israeli cities. Its main street, Dizengoff, sports numerous chic cafés, restaurants, shops and galleries. So famous is the street within Israel, that its name has been incorporated into the language. The Hebrew verb "l'hisdangev", meaning to parade down Dizengoff, describes the particularly Israeli custom of strolling down the street while watching and being watched by passers-by. So if your particular phobia is the feeling of being followed by countless eyes, stay away from Dizengoff!

Tel Aviv also offers the visitor long stretches of golden beach, and its hotels provide even the most discerning of customers with the kind of quality and service they would expect from any international city.

For those who grow tired of the lazy beach existence, Tel Aviv offers plenty to stimulate the intellect. The city is literally strewn with museums. One of the most recent and interesting is the Beit Hatefutzot — the museum of the Diaspora – which stands in the grounds of Tel Aviv University campus. This tells of the fragmented but powerful history of the Jewish people in the lands to which they were exiled. Nearby,

Preceding page Tel Aviv's lively Atarim Square at night.

Right Tel Aviv sports some of the finest hotels in the world. Perched by the Mediterranean shore, they allow the visitor to take full advantage of the nearby beach while still enjoying all the facilities that a modern hotel has to offer.

Below Even vacationers have to take some time off from the ardors of sunbathing! Beach cafés provide the essential refreshments, and of course the opportunity to discuss the day's news.

and within the same complex, one can see the Museums of Science and Technology and Glass and Ceramics.

Tel Aviv is also the home of the Habima National Theater and the Israeli Philharmonic Orchestra. These, together with the nightclubs and cinemas with which Tel Aviv is well endowed, ensure that a stay in this city will not be a quiet one.

Jaffa, which lies next to Tel Aviv, has a totally different flavor. The town has a long and ancient history and there are many myths and legends concerning it. Its name is a derivative of the Hebrew word "yafo", meaning beautiful, although a competing legend states that it was named after Noah's son Japhet, who it is claimed founded the city after the floods. Yet another legend, from Greek mythology, claims that Jaffa is the site where the beautiful princess Andromeda was rescued from the monster of the sea by Perseus, who slew the monster and unshackled the fair maiden. Whichever legend is true, it is certain that set high on a hill overlooking the sea, Jaffa is a truly beautiful town.

Today's visitor need not fear the possibility of being ravaged by a sea monster. The town contains a quiet Artists' Quarter, where one can observe the artists at work in their studios. The ancient harbor, which in biblical times was the main industrial port of the Israelite kingdom, is today a quaint fishing harbor surrounded by cafés and restaurants. Its commercial life has only recently ended. During the British mandate Jaffa was an important port, and it was here that many of the Jewish immigrants disembarked. In 1968 a modern deep water port was opened at Ashdod, and this ended the commercial usefulness of Israel's oldest port.

Below Not to be outdone by other major cities in the world, Tel Aviv also boasts a modern marina. For Israelis who can afford it the Mediterranean offers ideal sailing conditions and a perfect way in which to relax after the stresses and strains of everyday life.

Right One of the Dizengoff cafés for which Tel Aviv is so famous. It is here that Israelis attempt to solve the world's problems! Dizengoff is also Israel's fashion center and one can quite happily spend an evening observing the latest fashions on parade.

Below Modern agricultural and irrigation techniques have transformed Israel into the "Land of Milk and Honey" described in the Bible. Her agricultural products are sold all over the world and are a key component in the national economy. However within Israel vegetables are plentiful, delicious and inexpensive.

Another sea town with an important history is that of Caesarea. Positioned midway between Haifa and Tel Aviv, Caesarea is both an archaeologist's dream and a sportsman's delight. You can lie on golden beaches seeking occasional respite from the heat of the sun under the arches of an ancient Roman aqueduct; you can dive into the cool and refreshing sea from the pier of the Roman/Crusader harbor; and you can play golf on a modern course to the accompaniment of classical music echoing from the restored Roman amphitheater.

Caesarea was founded in the third century by the Phoenicians, and became an important city under the Romans. For 600 years it was the capital of the Roman province of Judea, and the visitor today can see extensive excavations showing the main features of the Roman city. It was also a fortress town under the Crusaders, although in spite of the formidable walls and moat which remain visible today, it was inevitably conquered and destroyed by the Islamic armies.

Following its destruction in 1265 AD, Caesarea faded from the map, submerged and forgotten under the sand dunes. It was only in 1940, with the founding of the nearby Kibbutz of Sdot Yam, that the area began to revive. Today the visitor can stay in the five star luxury of the neighboring hotel, or in the "no frills" atmosphere of the Kibbutz-run guest house. The restored pier is now the site of a romantic fish restaurant where one can eat surrounded by antiquity, and with the sound of the sea gently lapping against the pier's ancient foundations.

Left DRINK COCA COLA! In Israel's hot
climate this is indeed a pleasant invitation.
One might even try drinking it at the Israeli
version of MacDonalds, "MacDavids"!

Below This stylish building is in
fact a branch office of one of Israel's major
banking groups. In keeping with the modern
appearance, Israeli banks make full use of the
latest technology and can boast of a highly
computerized banking system.

Right Jaffa, which lies adjacent to Tel Aviv. The town has an ancient history and was once the main port in the region. In 1948 its Arab inhabitants fled and the city has now become a chic suburb of Tel Aviv with an important artists' colony.

Below Part of the Crusader port at Caesarea. This ancient town was also the capital of the Roman province of Judaea, and one can see in the picture some of the Roman columns which were later used by the Crusaders in building the port.

Left The view from the top of the hill on which Jaffa is built. In the background loom Tel Aviv's modern skyscrapers, contrasting sharply with the antiquity of Jaffa.

Below Jaffa's old and narrow streets boast many small and exquisite shops and restaurants. Until recently the harbor provided a refuge from the stormy seas. Now, having been restored, its cafés and restaurants provide the visitor with a different kind of refuge.

CHAPTER 4

Towns of the North

A short distance north of Caesarea lies the modern port of Haifa. Its harbor is equipped to handle ships of all shapes and sizes, from luxury liners to enormous modern oil tankers. Its quays are surrounded by warehouses, grain silos, container terminals, repair and servicing workshops and all the paraphernalia required by a modern port. During the British mandate a pipeline linked Iraqi oil fields with Haifa's oil refineries. Today the pipeline lies disused, but the oil refineries with their giant vats continue to process the oil required for Israel's internal use.

Haifa is built on the rugged slopes of the Carmel mountain range. The mountain's heights can be scaled in the relative comfort of Israel's only underground railway, the "Karmelit", although a good network of roads also connects the harbor area with its loftier suburbs. It's only from the top of the Carmel that one realizes why Haifa is such a popular residential as well as industrial city. The view that greets you is, without exaggeration, breathtaking. The expansive azure bay lies below in striking contrast to the verdant mountain slopes. At night a twinkling show of lights tumbles down to the edge of the coal black sea.

Taking advantage of this view, the small chic suburb which crowns the Carmel is populated by numerous intimate restaurants, fashionable jewelry and clothing shops and several of Haifa's luxury hotels.

Two points in particular strike the visitor's eye. The tall and elegant tower which stands two or three miles outside Haifa and high up on the Carmel range, marks the site of Haifa University. As with most of Israel's important towns however, the University is not the city's only institution of academic excellence. Its companion and rival, the Haifa Technion, has also established an international reputation for its academic

and scientific achievements.

The second focal point on the slopes of the Carmel is the stunning golden dome of the Bahai Temple, set amidst lush Persian gardens. The Bahai faith is a relatively new religion formulated by the prophet Bahaulah who died in Acre in 1892. The faith, which stresses the unity of God and the brotherhood of Mankind has, in spite of its late start, more than a million adherents scattered around the world.

A few miles north of Haifa lies one of the world's oldest cities, Acre. Jutting into the Mediterranean, its domes and minarets seem to hover over the gently swelling sea. Although mentioned in the Bible, Acre's commercial importance began with its conquest by the Crusaders in 1104 AD. It became their main port and for many years was the capital of the Crusader kingdom. Totally destroyed in 1291 by the conquering

Mamelukes, it was only in 1740, after 450 years of desolation, that Acre was again rebuilt as the political capital of the country. Because of its strategic importance, Acre continued to be a much fought-over city. Perhaps the most dramatic attempted conquest was that by Napoleon in 1799, who was soundly defeated with the help of the British fleet.

Today Acre is a quiet fishing town. The advent of the steam boat in the latter part of the eighteenth century destroyed its commercial usefulness, favoring the larger and better-equipped harbors of Haifa and Beirut. However, the visitor is constantly reminded of the city's vigorous past as he wanders down its narrow lanes and byways. Parts of the Crusader city have been discovered several feet underneath the present town, and the remains provide a unique insight into the life of the Crusader

Preceding pages The ancient city of Acre, once the country's capital.

Facing page A panoramic view of Haifa from the Bahai temple on the slopes of Mount Carmel. The temple itself marks the burial site of Mirza Ali Muhammed – known as "El Bab" – who was the founder of the Bahai faith and who was shot in 1850.

Below North from Acre lies a stretch of unspoilt coastline, often exposed to violent storms. In past times this coast was fearfully risky for all shipping.

Below The Crypt of St John is one of the best preserved Crusader churches in Israel. The Crypt is part of an extensive "underground" city lying beneath the present street level. Much of the Crusader city has been excavated and is now open to the public.

Right The quiet fishing harbor is central to the history of Acre. Founded in biblical times, it was an important fishing and trading center. Both the Crusaders and Turks appreciated its strategic and commercial importance and under the rule of both, Acre became the capital city of the region.

Right A view of the "Al Jazzar" mosque in Acre. Named after its founder, Jazzar Pasha, the mosque was built in 1781 on the ruins of the Crusader cathedral. The mosque is the largest and one of the most important in the country.

Facing page Acre's port, which was once the site of a fierce sea battle, is now a quiet fishing harbor. The noisiest it ever becomes is when it is invaded by Israeli children as part of their sea scout training.

conquerors. The Turkish citadel, now a hospital, is a reminder of a different period when Jewish freedom fighters were imprisoned and, in some cases, executed by the British authorities. The visitor will also see the beautiful eighteenth century mosque constructed by Ahmed al-Jazzar Pasha when he rebuilt the town. Above all, the overriding quality of Acre is its old world charm, its lively and noisy markets contrasting with its quiet and peaceful harbor, where the visitor can sit and sip a drink while contemplating the fierce battles that have, in times past, ravaged the town.

Inland from Acre, high in the hills of the Galilee, lies another ancient town, that of Safed. During the many years of Jewish exile, Safed became an important religious center and is particularly renowned as the home of the "Cabbala" or Jewish Mysticism. Today the town with its population of about 15 000 remains an important religious center. The fresh

mountain air and the splendid views of the surrounding hills and valleys have also attracted a large number of artists. The roaming visitor is consequently greeted by an array of small galleries nestling quietly amongst ancient and holy synagogues.

Strolling through the town, the visitor might be forgiven for failing to notice the small harmless looking cannon in its center. The homemade cannon, named the "Davidka", played a crucial role in the 1948 War of Independence. Surrounded by hostile Arab forces, the Jewish defenders improvised by using the "Davidka" to create a terrifying noise. The Arab attackers, believing that the Jewish forces were in possession of an atomic bomb, fled in disarray and the town survived with relatively few casualties.

South of Safed lies the mainly Arab town of Nazareth. Resting in a basin in the hills, modern Nazareth is a town of contrasts. Arab cafés line the streets with men seated

outside in their traditional costumes smoking the oriental pipe, the "nargillah", through a bubbling bowl of scented water. From within the lively sounds of eastern music waft into the street, while outside men concentrate on the game of "shesh-besh", an ancient form of backgammon.

It is for its Christian past rather than its exotic cafés that Nazareth is known. Here it was that Joseph worked as a carpenter, and where Mary received the Annunciation that she was to give birth to the Messiah. Jesus spent much of his childhood here and today many of the places associated with Jesus' life in the town are marked and remembered by a wealth of holy sites. The holiest shrine, the site of the Annunciation, is marked by a grand new Basilica, covering the remains of previous churches.

The ancient well known as "Mary's Well" is still used by local residents, and close to the town is the church of Kafr Kanna where Jesus is said to have performed the miracle

Right Named after the Roman Emperor Tiberius, the city of Tiberias was for many years one of the main Jewish religious centers of the Holy Land. Sited on the shores of the Sea of Galilee, Tiberias must be among the most beautiful places in the world.

Below Perched at the top of the Mount of Beatitudes the Franciscan church commands a dramatic view over the Sea of Galilee. The church marks the site at which Jesus made his Sermon on the Mount in which he said, "Blessed are the meek: for they shall inherit the earth".

of "the water that was made wine".

Lying to the south of Nazareth are the remains of Megiddo. It is easy to see why this was at one time an important strategic site. From the battlements that once existed, the commander of the Megiddo garrison would have been able to dominate the Valley of Jezreel and the important road connecting ancient Egypt with Syria and Mesopotamia. Even in modern times Megiddo has been of strategic importance and it was through the Megiddo Pass that the Allied armies under General Allenby invaded Palestine in 1918.

Today the site that was once so well fortified lies in ruins. Although of archaeological interest, it is Christian folklore that gives Megiddo its significance and notoriety. For it's here that Armageddon, the final battle between good and evil, is predicted to occur. Looking at the fertile vineyards and orchards which surround the ruins, it's difficult to imagine that Megiddo might one day be the epicenter of the world's destruction.

Above The Chapel of St Peter on its quiet hilltop site overlooking the Sea of Galilee. Its domes recall the architecture of Crusader times.

Left A Druze farmer on the Golan Heights. An offshoot of Islam, the Druze are a religious sect formed about 850 years ago. Druze are loyal to the State of Israel and serve in the Israeli army.

Preceding pages A view over the Sea of Galilee. The fresh-water lake, which is full of a variety of fish, is also known as Lake Kinneret, from the Hebrew word for a harp (the sea is shaped like a harp). It was on the Kinneret that Jesus is said to have "walked on the stormy water".

Below A typical Druze family. The Druze religion is shrouded in mystery. Originating in the eleventh century, it is based on the claim of Al Hakim, Khaliph of Egypt, to being the reincarnation of the deity. The religion itself was established in Northern Arabia by Ismail Al-Darazi, a follower of the Khaliph. The Druze religious doctrines are known only by the elders of the sect.

Right A Druze house in one of the villages in Northern Israel.

Facing page below Safed lies high up in the mountains of Upper Galilee more than 3000 feet (1000 meters) above sea level. Once the home of the "Cabbalists", a group of religious Jewish mystics, Safed still retains numerous small and enchanting synagogues.

Left Safed is now the home of a thriving artists' community. Its attractive streets are relatively new, having been built after the town was destroyed by an earthquake in 1837. The same earthquake was also responsible for damage to Tiberias.

Below A view of the modern Church of the Annunciation in Nazareth. Designed by the Italian architect Muzio, the church encloses the remains of earlier churches, parts of which have been restored and are now visible from within the church.

Desert Landscapes

Israel's landscape changes dramatically over fairly short distances. South of Nazareth and East of Jerusalem lies the Judean desert. It is a complete contrast to the fertile hills of the Galilee. Narrow treacherous roads wind themselves down steep rocky ravines. After a rain storm or flash flood some greenery emerges, but quickly shrivels in the merciless desert sun.

It is in this inhospitable environment that the rock of Masada is sited. It's a dramatic sight, jutting out of the Judean desert and towering over the calm of the Dead Sea. It was at Masada that Herod built himself a luxurious winter palace equipped with formidable defences. These defences were used in the first Jewish revolt against the Romans in 70 AD. After five years of open rebellion the Jewish insurrection was crushed and Jerusalem destroyed. A small band of Zealots were however able to escape from Jerusalem and take refuge in the fortress palace at Masada. From this strategic base the Zealots continued their fight by raiding and harassing the Roman forces. It took the Romans more than two years to destroy this final outpost of rebellion. Rather than submit to the ignominy of defeat the Zealots burnt down their belongings and holy buildings and then put themselves to death. Remarkably, almost 1900 years later, archaeologists were able to re-discover the very skeletons and possessions burnt by the Zealots in their last act of defiance.

The Roman victory at Masada did not end Jewish resistance to Roman rule. In 132 AD the Jews again rose up against their Roman overlords and under the leadership of Simon Bar Kochba were able to form an independent state which survived for almost three years. It was again in the numerous caves which surround the area that the Jewish insurgents sought shelter when the tide of war inevitably turned

Preceding pages The Israeli camel corps on patrol in the Negev desert.

Right Lying 1306 feet (398 meters) below sea level, the DeadSea is the largest lake in Israel. Because of the density of the salt in the water, bathers in the sea can enjoy the sensation of floating effortlessly while tanning themselves in the sun.

Below The water in the Dead Sea is the most salt saturated in the world. While ordinary water holds approximately 5 per cent solids, that in the Dead Sea holds about 26 per cent. The picture shows salt crystals and the skeletons of trees covered with salt.

against them. And it was from these caves, and those at Qumran, that numerous ancient artifacts, including the Dead Sea Scrolls, were found.

Today's visitor will not have the same difficulties that the Romans had in exploring the area. One can reach the top of Masada in the relative luxury of a cable car, although the more adventurous may prefer the arduous climb along the snaking path which winds its way up the steep slopes of the mountain. Once at the top there is a spectacular view over the Dead Sea and into Jordan, and if you climb the rock before dawn you'll catch the sun rising in a fiery ball over the flat white-salted water. The springs of Ein Gedi are close by and this hidden oasis provides a refreshing contrast to the dry desert landscape of Masada. The Dead Sea itself might attract many an overheated visitor, and although it's fun to experience the sensation of floating without effort, the salty water will quickly find its way into and irritate the small scratches you never knew you had! Those who aren't

concerned with outward appearances might try the nearby sulfur baths which are supposed to have a highly therapeutic effect. But being covered in black mud certainly ensures that glamor pays no part in the proceedings!

The Dead Sea area is not just important for its historical significance. Sited at the edge of the sea is the "solar pond project" which, by using space age technology, is already producing enough electricity to power a hotel.

Traveling south of the Dead Sea and deeper into the Negev, technology continues to have an impact on the landscape. Although in Roman times the Negev desert was inhabited, under Arab rule which commenced in 630 AD, the Negev became a desolate no-man's land. It was only in 1948, with the creation of the state of Israel, that the Negev began to revive. Today the visitor might not realize that he has in fact entered the desert. Use of advanced irrigation techniques, which make full use of the salt water lying underground, have today transformed the area into a fertile agricultural region. Beersheva, the capital of the Negev, was until recently a small outpost town in the middle of the desert. It has now changed into a modern city surrounded by kibbutz and moshav farms. Linked to the industrial heartland of the country by modern motorways, it has its own expanding university which specializes in agricultural research in desert climates.

South of Beersheva even Israeli technology cannot disguise the fact that one has entered a desert region, although isolated and fertile settlements appear at frequent intervals along the roadside. In spite of the harsh conditions, sizeable towns have developed. Eilat, the largest and most southern, has a population in excess of 20 000. It is a thriving resort town, offering its visitors year-round sunshine, the beauty of the Red Sea, and excellent facilities for deep sea diving and water sports of all kinds. It's also an important port and is connected to the north of Israel by a pipeline. Tin is mined nearby and one can still see the site of the mines used by King Solomon more than 2000 years ago. Eilat also has an extraordinary underwater gallery, through which one can view the sea inhabitants which feed on the nearby reef. Surrounded by all of these achievements, it is sometimes difficult to remember that less than 40 years ago there was no more than a solitary hut on the site of all this industry. Yet, as with the rest of this remarkable country, so much has been achieved in what in comparison to the ancient history of the land is a very short space of time.

Below A desert scene in the Negev close to Eilat. The mountains in the distance are Jordanian territory. Plants survive the desert climate by growing their roots so deep that they reach down to underground water.

Left A "wadi" in the Negev desert. "Wadis" are created by rain water. It rains for only one or two days a year in the desert, but when it does the water rushes down from the mountain tops, cutting paths through the hard rock.

Below Bedouin collecting water from a well in the Negev desert. Water is the most scarce commodity in the desert environment. Without it the desert would quickly become uninhabitable, even for the Bedouin who are well accustomed to its hardships.

Right South of Eilat and well into the Sinai desert lies this enchanting desert landscape: the inlet looks more characteristic of the Scandinavian coast line and is accordingly referred to as the "fjord".

Below A vacation spot on the coast of the Red Sea. The Red Sea resorts are well known for providing their guests with comfortable seclusion from the rest of the world. They are also known as havens for those who prefer to bathe "au naturel".

Left The library buildings of Ben Gurion University in Beersheva. Beersheva has been transformed from a small shanty town into a modern industrial city providing essential services for the numerous agricultural communities surrounding it.

Below The Dead Sea Works at the southern tip of the Dead Sea. The sea's high mineral content provides a useful source of salt, asphalt and sulfur. All three minerals are used in a wide variety of industrial processes.

Overleaf A lone tree struggles in the desert sun. Thirty years ago most of the Negev looked like this. Today, however, numerous agricultural settlements, using drip irrigation techniques, have begun to transform the landscape.

53

A Little Miracle

The visitor to Israel might be surprised to know quite how small this significant country is. Its area measures 12 905 square miles (20 770 square kilometers) and it is a little larger than the state of New Jersey. If one compares it to the total size of the USA then Israel is a minuscule 0.002 times the size. Prior to the Six Day War Israel was actually only nine miles wide at one particular point. Today however, with the extra territory of the West Bank, Israel is slightly wider, although one is rarely more than a two hour drive from her border. In ancient times the Israelite Kingdom lay on the important trading route between Egypt in the south and Syria and Mesopotamia in the north. Israel still lies in an important trading position today. She has ports on both the Red Sea and the Mediterranean and is ideally situated for trading with Europe, North Africa, Asia, and, if there were to be peace, with Arabia. She is also sited in an important strategic position and can offer her allies useful facilities for their various Mediterranean and Middle Eastern activities.

In spite of her varied and contrasting landscapes, Israel lacks one vital element. With the exception of salt, Israel has few mineral resources. Israelis joke that if Moses had turned to the right and not to the left, Israel would today be sited on some of the richest oil fields in the world. The fact of the matter is, though, that Israel is obliged to import almost all of her energy and raw material requirements. This is only one of the burdens that the Israeli economy has to bear. Surrounded by hostile states, Israel is subjected to a trade boycott by almost all of her neighbors and is obliged to spend a very high proportion of her national product on defense measures.

In such difficult circumstances it is hardly surprising that the Israeli economy is under great pressure. Visitors will notice

Preceding pages Follow the arrow for coffee!

Right As an alternative to army service conscripts can choose to do voluntary work, although they remain attached to the army and still undergo basic military training. Here a young soldier feeds chickens as part of her voluntary service.

Below Water-melons being boxed for export. A lot of research goes into Israeli agricultural production and this has recently helped to produce a new fruit: a cross between a tomato and a peach.

that even the newspapers they buy change in price from day to day, and that to avoid the problems of such rapid inflation most prices are in fact quoted in US dollars. With an inflation rate that has exceeded 400 per cent, one might well wonder how the average Israeli survives. The trick, it would seem, is to rush to the shops on pay day and to buy the month's requirements. If one waits, even for a day, the prices will have risen and the value of one's pay check considerably declined.

There is, however, a bright side to the story. Israel has one resource to which no value can be applied; the brain power of her residents. Education is one of Israel's main priorities. For a state with a population slightly greater than four million, Israel has seven universities and in 1983 had more than 60 000 students. This concern for education produces results and Israel today specializes in a whole range of high technology industries. Recently, for example, a technique has been developed for growing plants in the air. Instead of being cultivated in rows of plowed fields, the plants grow in sealed troughs where their exposed roots receive nutrient-enriched mist from an advanced computer-controlled spray system.

Left An army reservist helps to cook the evening meal. Reserve duty is a necessary part of everyday life for Israeli men. They are required to give at least one month a year to the army and in times of trouble considerably more. This is the only way that Israel can even begin to match the manpower available to those Arab states hostile to her.

Below A "kibbutznik" and his dog plough up a field of waste ground.

Below Israeli soldiers in town. Living in the midst of terrorist attacks, soldiers are visible throughout Israel. Even when traveling home they are under orders to carry their rifles at all times so that they are never caught unprepared.

It is perhaps in the field of medicine that Israel has made the largest strides. She is today one of the leading countries in the production of new generation scanners and laser equipment. It is because of the massive technological strides that Israeli industry is constantly making, that the industrial world ultimately trusts in her economic survival. And Israelis, in spite of the harsh economic climate in which they find themselves, know that they will always be able to find export markets for their ingenious and modern products.

One of Israel's most advanced industries has been so successful that it is almost taken for granted. The control of Israel's limited water resources is of crucial importance to the country. A national water grid pumps and distributes this precious commodity to its agricultural and industrial consumers. Each large consumer is granted a specific allocation in order to insure that everyone receives a quantity of

Right A woman tank commander training in the Negev. The Israeli army is a highly mobile force and depends heavily on its armored corps. As a result Israel now manufactures her own tank which has been specifically designed to suit the country's needs.

water appropriate to their needs. The success of the system can easily be seen as the visitor travels around the country. Fields are green and fertile and on occasions it's easy to forget that one is traveling in a very hot climate over land that was in most places desert only 40 years ago.

It was the young men and women who worked and often died in the fields who must be thanked for Israel's agricultural transformation. Arriving from the ghettos in Eastern and Central Europe, these young pioneers resolved to build a new society based on manual work and communal living. The first kibbutz, Degania, was founded in 1909 in the Jordan Valley south of the Sea of Galilee. As with so many other kibbutzim, the ground on which it was sited had been sold to the settlers as it was thought to be impossible to farm, and was totally uninhabitable. The land had been a swamp for centuries and was malaria-infested. In spite of the difficulties, the

Left A father happy to be home after his "milluim", reserve duty. To Westerners a man holding a gun and a baby may seem incongruous, but not to Israelis. It is the gun that protects the family from those determined to destroy it.

Below A mother mourns her son. In such a small country there are few families who have not suffered a loss from one of Israel's five wars.

young kibbutzniks dug canals and drained the land. They succeeded in removing all signs of the swamps and created a fertile agricultural settlement on land that had previously been considered as unusable.

Today the kibbutzim are no longer struggling and impoverished settlements but highly successful agricultural communities. While primarily based on agriculture, they have also established industries in a variety of different areas. One new kibbutz, for instance, specializes in the production and repair of dentures, while others concentrate on more traditional tasks such as the production of tiles, and carpentry. It is, however, in the social structure of their communities that the kibbutzim have had most success. The original ideals of the founding members have been maintained and indeed carried forward. Private ownership has been abolished and all the income earned by the kibbutz members is pooled and used for

communal purposes. Within the kibbutz itself money is not used, and in fact not needed. Everything is provided free of charge to the commune's members. Food, accommodation, child care and education are given to each according to his or her needs. Some aspects of this communal life are still considered controversial today. For instance, children in many kibbutzim sleep in children's houses. During the working day they are looked after by well-trained child minders. In spite of the controversy that still surrounds this form of upbringing, parents are able to spend their leisure time enjoying the company of their children knowing that during working hours their offspring are being given the very best in child care and education.

There are today more than 200 kibbutzim in Israel, with a population in excess of 130000. They nevertheless represent only a small proportion of the country's population. Their small numbers disguise their immense importance to the country. They are not only the economic and industrial backbone of the nation: they have provided Israel with some of her greatest political leaders and produce a very high proportion of the officers within the army and air force. These small communities of idealistic people continue to give Israel the moral and political leadership which has been so essential to her survival in the hostile world she finds herself inhabiting.

Below Kibbutz Degania is known today as the "mother of Kibbutzot". Surrounded by fertile fields where once there were swamps, the kibbutz has retained a burnt-out Syrian tank as a reminder of the threat still posed to Israel by her neighbors.

Left This ingenious machine is a gas-fueled crane used to pick fruit from the tallest of trees. Here it is being used in a more casual role during a kibbutz race.

Below Israeli children must be the most pampered in the world. In particular, parents place a high priority on learning and this is reflected in the large proportion of state funds devoted to education.

Left The secret of Israel's agricultural success lies in her irrigation techniques. Permanent pipes are laid (as shown here) from the main water supply to a terminal in each field and from there to each plant by rubber piping.

Preceding pages Fish farming is an agricultural activity not normally associated with Israel, or indeed the Middle East in general. These fresh-water lakes are at the edge of the Sea of Galilee and produce silver carp and St Peter's fish.

Facing page One of the roads that winds its way through the Judean Hills. The road runs from Jerusalem in the west towards the Dead Sea in the east.

Left The Armenian quarter in the Old City of Jerusalem is a walled city within a walled city. The compound is inhabited by 5000 people and maintains its own schools and institutions. The quarter is built around the Church of St James the Great but also contains other important churches and institutions.

Below In spite of the technological advances constantly being made by Israeli scientists, some old customs never die. The donkey remains, as ever, a reliable although stubborn and slow form of transport. Speed, however, is not essential while tending goats!

Facing page A Yemenite bride dressed in a traditional wedding costume. The old customs of the various Jewish communities differ greatly although all share common fundamental beliefs.

Left A Yemenite bride being prepared for her wedding. Israelis are very marriage-orientated and tend to marry at a much younger age than is common in most other Western countries. As a result Israel's birth rate is also quite high.

Below Israeli folk dancers dressed in traditional costumes. Folk dancing is a popular pastime, particularly with the young. Most schools make facilities available and in the summer many groups take to the open air. It is not difficult for beginners to master the basic steps and the dancing is enormous fun.

Things to see in Israel

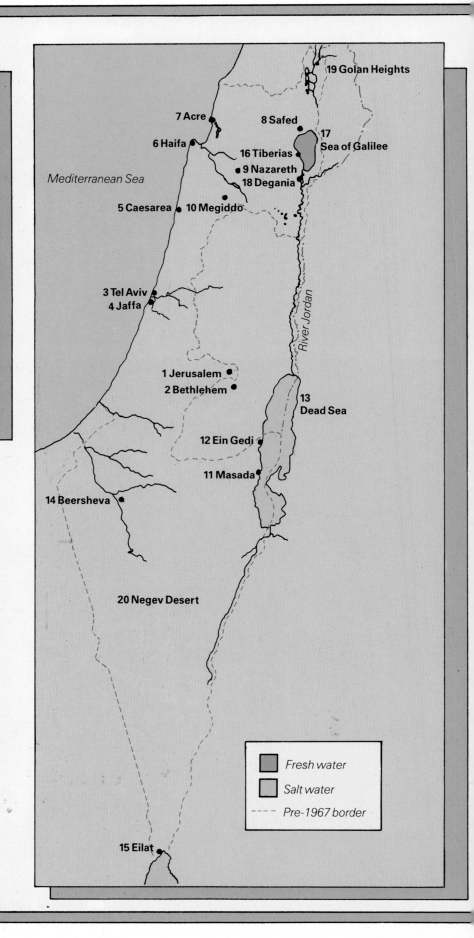

1 Jerusalem The capital of Israel whose Hebrew name Yerushalayim means "Town of Peace". Contains some of the most holy places of Judaism, Christianity and Islam.

2 Bethlehem Lies south of Jerusalem. Its name means "House of Bread" and refers to the surrounding fertile countryside. The church, built by the Emperor Justinus in 614, stands on the site where Christ was born.

3 Tel Aviv The commercial and cultural center of the country. Its name means "Spring Hill" and it stands on the Mediterranean in Israel's most densely populated region.

4 Jaffa One of the oldest cities in the world, and now a suburb of Tel Aviv. With its narrow lanes, stair streets, cafes, artists' studios, markets and nightclubs, it is well worth seeing.

5 Caesarea An important excavation site with its magnificent Roman amphitheater – the setting for concerts – with the Mediterranean as a backdrop. The home of Israel's only golf course!

6 Haifa Israel's largest seaport and the center of Israeli commerce and industry. On the forested slopes of Mt Carmel, Haifa is said to be one of most beautiful cities in the world.

7 Acre Standing north of Haifa at the end of the Bay of Haifa, Acre is one of the oldest and historically greatest seaports of the world. The Old City is an impressive museum of Islamic and Crusader art.

Tel Aviv

Sea of Galilee

Bethlehem

Jerusalem

Masada

Dead Sea

13 Dead Sea The lowest point on earth, at 1306 feet (398 meters) below sea level. The salt content is so dense that one can sit or lie on it motionless without sinking. The sea also has a series of radioactive springs which are used for health purposes.

8 Safed Lying on the slopes of Mt Canaan, Safed is well known for its picturesque artists' quarter as well as its many beautiful synagogues. An important holy town for the Jews with its cabbalist associations.

9 Nazareth After Jerusalem and Bethlehem, Nazareth is the center of Christian pilgrimages in Israel. The home of Joseph and Mary, Old Nazareth is an Arab town, dominated by the magnificent Church of the Annunciation.

10 Megiddo One of the most significant sites in Israel. Megiddo stood on the ancient trade and army route between Egypt and Mesopotamia, and has always been an important strategic site.

11 Masada Masada means "fortress" and the fortress ruins stand on a 1200-foot (400-meter) high plateau overlooking the Dead Sea. Built by Herod, it was the scene of mass suicide by over 900 Zealots who preferred to die rather than surrender to the Romans.

12 Ein Gedi A hidden oasis which rises above the Dead Sea. David's Waterfall plunges about 300 feet (100 meters) down from the boulders. It is home for the ibex and other remarkable fauna and flora.

14 Beersheva The capital of the Negev and, apart from archaeological excavations, noteworthy as the home of Ben Gurion University, and a museum with specialist interest in the surrounding Bedouin culture.

15 Eilat On the northern tip of the Gulf of Aqaba – on the opposite side of the bay is the Jordanian sea port of Aqaba. A developing tourist center – the sun shines all the year – with a wide variety of water sports, and a fascinating marine life.

16 Tiberias On the western shore of the Sea of Galilee, it is one of the holy places of Judaism as well as a holiday and health resort. The views over the Sea of Galilee and out on to the Golan Heights on the opposite shore are magnificent.

17 Sea of Galilee Israel's largest freshwater lake, also known as Lake Kinneret and Lake Tiberias, resembles a harp in shape. The river Jordan flows through Tiberias from the north to the south. Excellent for swimming, fishing and sailing.

18 Degania A kibbutz about 6 miles (10 km) south of Tiberias in the Jordan Valley. It was the first kibbutz to be established in Palestine, in 1909. At the time the area was a malaria-infested swamp.

19 Golan Heights Before the 1967 war the Heights were part of Syria, but today a 12-15 mile (20-25 km) wide strip belongs to Israel. The scene of fierce fighting in that war as the Heights look down upon the Israeli Huleh Valley which was constantly shelled by the Syrians.

20 Negev The Negev Desert consists of mountains, gorges, plateaus, wadis, dunes and oases, as well as sand! Water piped in from the north has ensured that the desert has bloomed, with kibbutzim and other settlements establishing agricultural bases in the area.

PICTURE CREDITS